# A SOFIA SPECIAL

Written by
## Julie Falatko

Illustrated by
## Vivian Mineker

chronicle books · san francisco

"I love dancing.

It makes me feel free.

Happy kick, spinny twirl,

I say hi to the—**WHOA**."

Sofia was dancing to school, as usual, when she spotted a flower.

"Oh, do you want to go to school with me?" she asked.

Sofia put the flower in her pocket.

"Do you like my dancing? I'm completely self-taught," she said.

"Today is Switcheroo Day," said
Ms. Junebeam. "Find your new seat!"

Sofia usually sat by the window.

"You would have liked the window," she told her flower.

Now Sofia was sitting by the sink—and getting wet.

"I'll protect you, little flower. There, is that better?" she said.

Ms. Junebeam clapped three times.
"Line up for gym class," she said.

"Who likes to dance?"
asked Mr. Hockenspocker.

"**ME!**" said Sofia.

"Today we will learn the
ancient art of square dancing,"
said Mr. Hockenspocker.

Sofia loved dancing, but her squares looked more like trapezoids.

"Here, kid," said Mr. Hockenspocker. "You can be the caller."

"It's okay. Recess will be fun,"
she told her flower.

Sofia waited her turn for the swings.
She loved to feel the wind, and she knew
her flower would too.

"Whee—**OUCH!**" said Sofia.

Sofia did her best to patch the hole in her tights.

"Today is bumpier than usual," she told her flower.
"Don't worry, lunch is next. You'll love lunch."

But at lunch, Sofia dropped her sandwich, and she didn't want to eat everyone's shoe germs.

"I'll share my sandwich with you," said Ellie.
"Your sandwich is a flower!" said Sofia.

"My mom knows I like my lunch in fun shapes," said Ellie.

"She can't see me eat a flower," whispered Sofia.

"I'm not sure she can actually see you at all," said Ellie.
"But I also have strawberries. Do you want some of these?"

"Yes, please," said Sofia.

"Exciting news, class," said Ms. Junebeam. "A group of dancers from the college is putting on an assembly this afternoon, and they are asking for five volunteers to do a modern dance with them."

Sofia wanted to be one of the volunteers. She loved dancing. Dancing made her feel free. But after everything, maybe the best thing to do was stand perfectly still in the middle of the room.

Or maybe not.

"My flower thinks I should say yes," Sofia said.

But her flower was wrong. The dance did not make her feel free. The dance made her feel confused.

"You are the mountain," the dance instructor guided.

"I'm the mountain?" asked Grover. "I thought I was Grover."

"Should this gong be louder?" asked Ellie, swinging the mallet.

"NOW CLIMB!" chanted the instructor.

"How can I climb the mountain if
I *am* the mountain?" Sofia asked.

On the way home, Sofia stepped, stomped, and twirled, but her heart wasn't in it.

"Today went sideways," Sofia told her flower.

A gust of wind lifted the flower out of her pocket and into the sky. Sofia watched her friend fly away.

"You dance better than I do," she said.

Soon she couldn't see her flower anywhere.

It was gone.

"Dad!" Sofia called. "I had a messy mountain of a day."

"I can tell," said her dad. "How about a Dad Special?"

"Yes, please," said Sofia. "I met a flower. But then we got wet, and I can't square-dance, we crash-landed, and my lunch went plop. Then I had to wear **THIS** onstage, and my flower flew away."

"That sounds like a lot," said her dad.

"It was," said Sofia.

She scooped ice cream into her bowl.

"How about you flip all those things around?" asked her dad.

Sofia pushed a raspberry into her mouth. "Like this?"

"I meant flip around all those parts of your day. What were some good things?"

"Hmm. It was sunny. I made a new friend," Sofia said. She added a berry for each of those good things.

"I built an excellent flower-protection shield." She added three more berries, because protecting her flower was important. She had been such a good flower protector that she decided to pop four more berries right into her mouth.

"And my tights do look very fashionable like this. Also, Ellie shared her strawberries, and I was brave." The berries were piled high, and she added eight more, until she couldn't see the ice cream underneath at all.

Best of all, I'm about to eat a Dad Special, which is a whole **MOUNTAIN OF BERRIES.**"

"Berry mountains are the best kind of mountain," said her dad.

Sofia scooped up some ice cream and a rainbow of berries. "Look, it's the perfect spoonful. I got some of everything," she said.

"Berries make everything better," said her dad.

She smiled and pushed the spoon into her mouth.
"This is a really yummy berry mountain."

"You have to be pretty strong to eat a whole mountain of berries," said her dad.

"And to smile at the end of a rough day."

"A Dad Special makes a bad day good, and a good day even better," said Sofia.

"Do you want to know a secret?" said her dad. "Sometimes it's not the Dad Special as much as who you're sharing it with. Maybe we should call it a Sofia Special."

"A Sofia Special?" she asked.

"Because it's as **SWEET** as you are," said her dad.

# MAKE YOUR OWN

Any day is a good day to share berries!

Ice cream

Scoop